Each book in this series is a thematic collection of words children use, words they see around them, and words for objects with which they are familiar.

Very young children will enjoy talking about the pictures and naming the items. Older children will be able to use the books as reference for their reading and writing, as well as for enjoyment.

Titles in this series
Me and Other People
Everyday Things
At Home
Things That Move
Places to Go

Also available as a Gift Box set

LADYBIRD BOOKS, INC., Lewiston, Maine 04240 U.S.A.
© LADYBIRD BOOKS LTD MCMLXXXVII
Loughborough, Leicestershire, England
Printed in England

things that move

compiled by LYNNE BRADBURY
illustrated by TERRY BURTON

Ladybird Books

Car

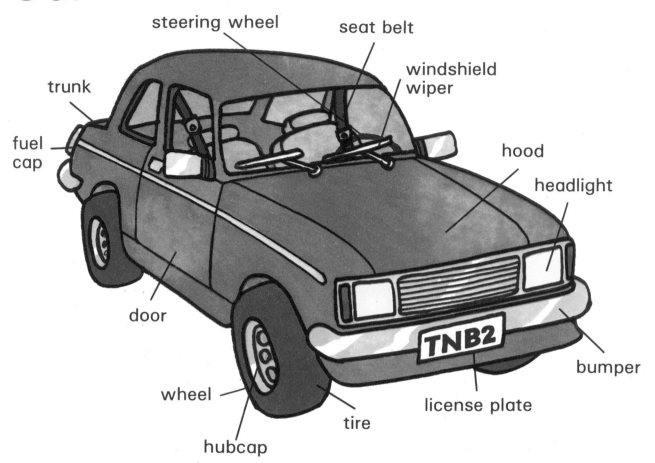

steering wheel

seat belt

windshield wiper

trunk

fuel cap

hood

headlight

door

wheel

hubcap

tire

TNB2

license plate

bumper

Tools

jack

wrench

oilcan

screwdriver

pliers

hammer

screws

Garage

cashier

bill

car sales

litter basket

gas pump

6

new and used cars

service and repairs

workshop

mechanic

air pressure pump

bucket

sponge

7

Other vehicles

panel truck

flat-bed truck

motorcycle

police car

land rover

POLICE

ambulance

bicycle

cement mixer

SHELL

tank truck

Trains

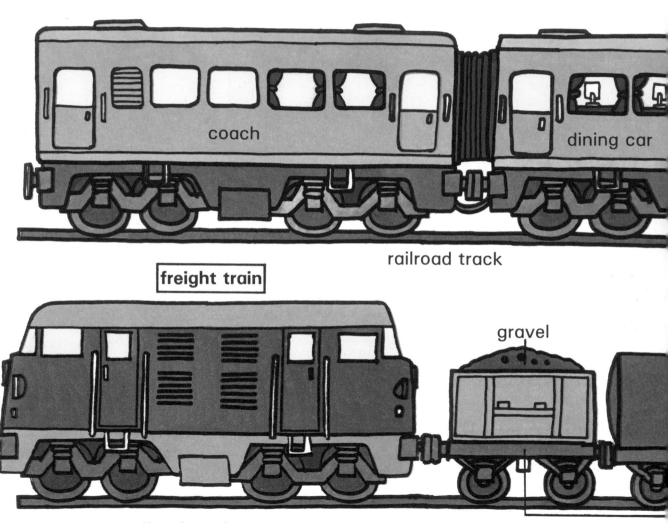

coach

dining car

railroad track

freight train

gravel

diesel engine

passenger train

tank car

sand

coal

caboose

cars

11

Railroad station

news

restaurant

waiting room

newsstand

conductor

passenger

suitcase

platform

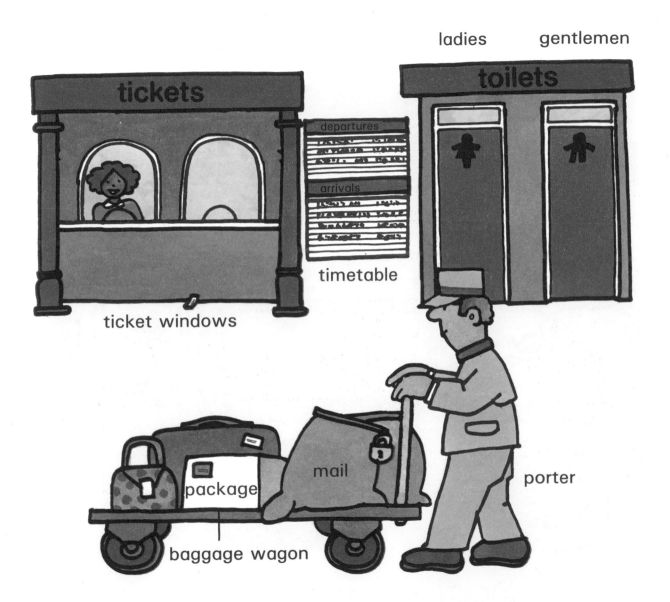

tickets

ladies   gentlemen

toilets

departures

arrivals

timetable

ticket windows

package

mail

porter

baggage wagon

13

Buses

exact change, please

driver

city bus

seat

driver

long-distance bus

wheel

Bus station

snack bar

bus stop

ticket office

bus fare

briefcase

shopping bag

handbag

Taxi

driver

taxi/
cab

meter

Boats and ships

harbor

tugboat

rope

cargo
ship

smokestack

crane

cargo

Docks

lighthouse

ocean

fishing boat

hovercraft

anchor

dock

ocean
liner

sailor

captain

2

Aircraft

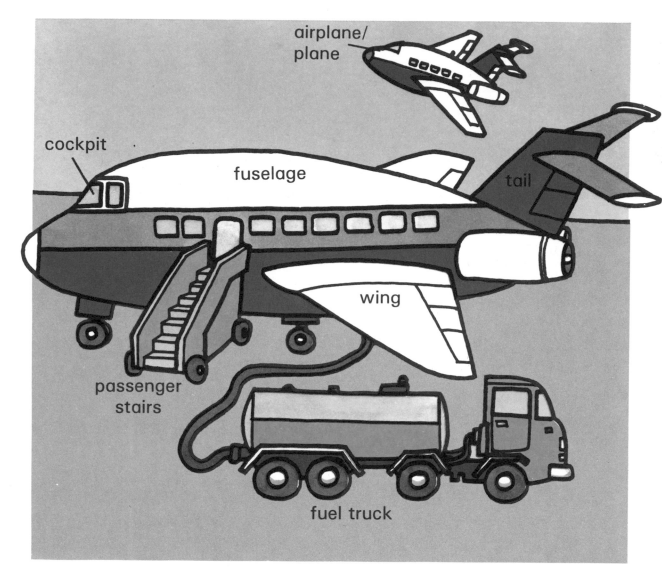

airplane/
plane

cockpit

fuselage

tail

wing

passenger
stairs

fuel truck

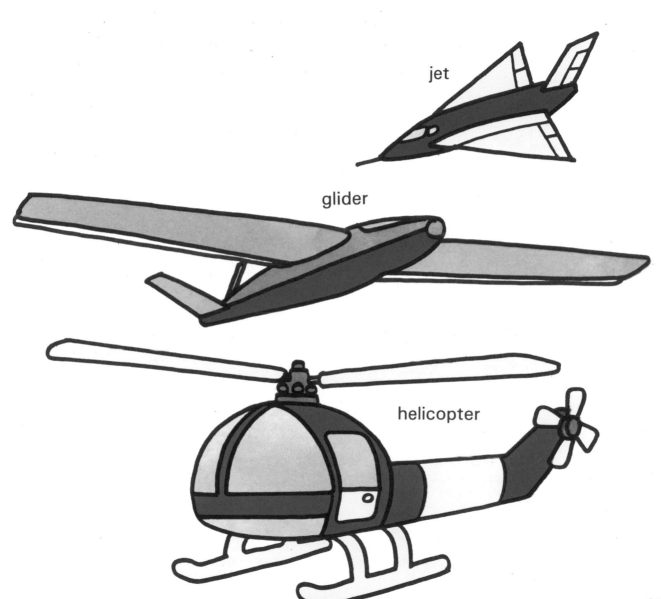

jet

glider

helicopter

23

Airport

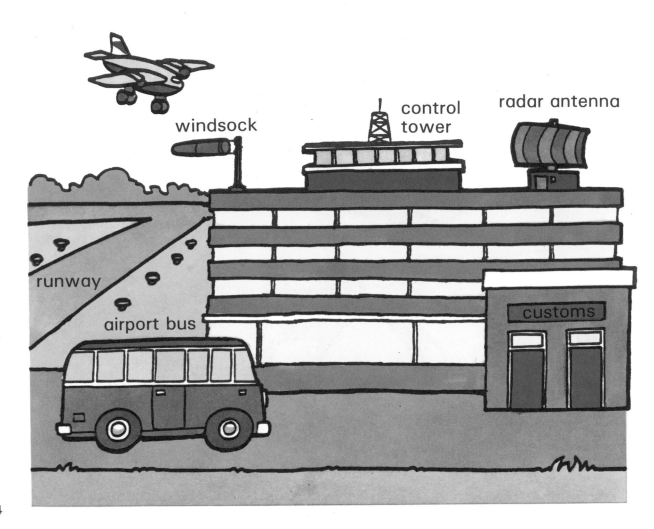

windsock

control tower

radar antenna

runway

airport bus

customs

Spacecraft

rocket

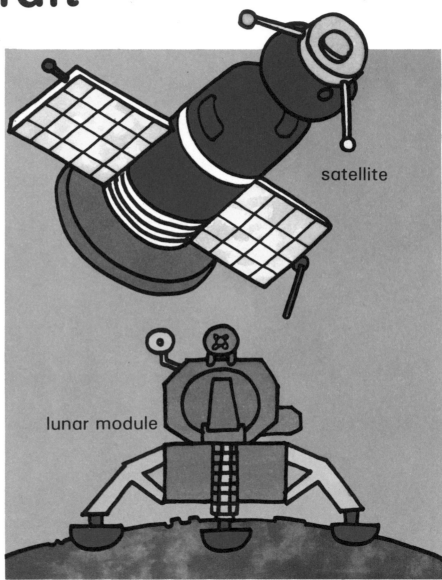

satellite

lunar module

helmet

space shuttle

planet

stars

astronaut

moon

27